M000033434

WHITE EAGLE'S
LITTLE BOOK OF
HEALING
COMFORT

WHITE EAGLE'S
Little Book of
Healing Comfort

WHITE EAGLE PUBLISHING TRUST
NEW LANDS · LISS · HAMPSHIRE · ENGLAND

First published September 2005

© *The White Eagle Publishing Trust, 2005*

**British Library
Cataloguing-in-Publication Data**
*A catalogue record for this book is available
from the British Library*

ISBN 0-85487-163-2

*This book is specially dedicated to White Eagle's
friends in the USA, in particular those who
have helped with its compilation*

*Set in Ehrhardt at the Publisher's and printed
and bound by Cambridge University Press*

FOREWORD

This little book of White Eagle's sayings, full of his timeless wisdom and philosophy, is offered in response to the great need for comfort and healing in this most challenging world. We trust that his gentle words, always clothed in warmth and deep understanding, will bring to you the realization that each one of us is truly a child of God, and is ever held safe in God's arms. All our needs are met when we remember this. In your quiet moments may you find that place of stillness and calm, and you will know beyond a shadow of a doubt, that all is *well*.

'*In the calmness of your spirit, try and retain the peace of heaven. Surrender yourself to the infinite love, wisdom and power of the Divine Master, the Great Healer, then you cannot fail to breathe in the breath of God and go forth to live in harmony with God's law. It is love.*'

WHITE EAGLE

CONTENTS

PREFACE

THE BRAVE SNOWDROP

They have pushed up through earth iron-hard with frost—these most tender and delicate and exquisite blooms. Neither winter's mud nor the battering of the hail has sullied their purity. They stand perfect in their humility, sustained by their steadfastness, as a pledge of brighter days to dawn for all the earth.

Maybe the soil out of which all the gentler things come forth is iron-hard in these days, and blustering storms and beating hail assail all tender growth in humanity. Yet delicate flowers of hope still arise, still hold forth a pledge that the eternal sequence will bring spring and sunshine from the winter of humanity's bitter discontent. 'I am the resurrection and the life', says the snowdrop; but it speaks with the voice of God, and all the powers of God uphold the flower and the promise it brings. So also with human kind, when it at last turns to God.

IVAN COOKE

From an editorial in the first White Eagle magazine, ANGELUS.

1

ENFOLDED
IN LOVE

COME INTO THE LIGHT

Look up and see the blazing heavenly light now pouring upon you, blessing you, filling your heart and mind. Surrender yourselves, surrender yourselves utterly to this blazing light, and the eternal wisdom, love and power of God—be *in* it. Your Father–Mother God knows your need, understands you, knows all the secret trials of your life. Surrender to the almighty Spirit. Come, come close, come closer to the Lord the Christ, who comes among you to bring you heavenly refreshment.

THE SWEETNESS WHICH
COMES FROM SPIRIT

Beloved, beloved, we bring to you a message, a truth about the power of love. You hear so much said about love. The spoken word seems to lose its power, but particularly we would bring to your hearts the emotion of love, the feeling of love. So cease thinking about your physical cares and your material anxieties, and concentrate upon the sweet, gentle emotion of love. We know that if you train yourselves to think in terms of love every moment of your life, you will find that unconsciously a beautiful healing will take place.

PEACE IS FOUND IN LISTENING

God has given unto the children of earth the gift of love, the gift of wisdom, which lies in the heart, and which is known by the name of 'the Spirit of Christ'. So cultivate the art of listening, in your quiet moments, to the spirit, and it will speak ever in one language, that of love. Love brings to your heart peace, kindliness and tolerance.

GOD IS BOTH FATHER AND MOTHER

The divine Motherhood of God can comfort all her children. Can you think of any greater love than that of a true mother? Therefore, how much greater must this love of the Divine Mother be for all on earth? Let us wonder at Her divinity, Her beauty and Her love.

IN THE ARMS OF GOD, ALL IS WELL

We want you to feel, as well as to see, broad wings of light, feathered wings expanding over the earth, radiating healing. Can you feel it yourselves, the simple pure power of God which is healing you, strengthening you, which is cleansing you from all ills? Nothing matters as much as you think it does on the material plane. You are here to learn this union with God, with Spirit. You have to learn to work and live and think all the time in that lovely Presence. It is there always.

LIFE LEADS TO UNDERSTANDING

May you all feel conscious … as never before in your lives, of the great inflow of the Christ Love. Never fear my brethren, God will never fail you, *never*. The difficulties which you have to endure are to lead you nearer to this great realization that life is spirit, and spirit is God, spirit is omnipotent, spirit overcometh all.

2

PEACE BE
IN YOUR HEART

FINDING THE SOURCE

When you are stressed and in pain, when you are fearful, anxious, and everything seems to be in a state of confusion for you. You know that when you can attune your thoughts to the Most High, your stresses fall away from you, and you find that you can at times touch the heart of peace. Now this, dear brethren, is the source of truth, the source of all healing: the heart of peace.

May this power flow through you, renewing all the life forces in you, new life, a fresh inflow of power and a wonderful peace.

PEACE, BE STILL

We speak words of peace to you all. Peace be with you; may nothing disturb the deep peace of Christ within. Humanity is learning—by slow degrees, but still learning—the way of life. Remember the storm, when the little boat was tossed upon the seas of emotion. But the Master was in command of the little craft, and He commanded the emotional storm to be still. So may Christ command your craft on the troublous seas of emotional strife. Be still, and know that God is Infinite Love. The clouds pass away.

GRACE

Put yourselves into harmony, into tune with spiritual law; and every need of your body, soul and spirit will be supplied. And what is this law? Divine Love! Keep your heart full of divine and gentle love. Keep control of your tongue, so that it says no unkind and hurtful thing. Remember the feelings of those to whom you speak, and so speak gently and thoughtfully without anger and without haste. Then difficulties fall away, sorrow recedes into the background, and you cannot help but know the gentle presence of your Master. As we remember Him, we are strengthened in loving kindness. We know nothing else in our hearts but compassion, sympathy and tenderness…. The peace which is beyond the understanding of the world enters, and He says, *My peace I leave with you; My peace I give unto you.*

STRENGTH WILL COME

Seek then for the quiet mind, for in the eternal peace of God your Father shall be your strength….

3

THE GENTLE HEALER

I WILL GIVE YOU ANOTHER COMFORTER

Beloved, we would draw a picture of the Presence of the Master Jesus, through whom flows the Great White Light. His form can be seen by those who attune themselves to his purity and love. His face is gentle, wise and strong, with deep blue eyes from which shines the wisdom of ages. His robe is white but glistening. He is clothed in the garments of the sun. His hands reach forth in the act of blessing each one of you. Thus, my children, may you feel His gentle, loving presence. He comes with love and blessing. He has promised.

MEDITATION ON CHRIST

You all have your own favourite picture of the Master Jesus. Many painters have tried to portray His heavenly beauty and grace. Few of these pictures satisfy the soul. If you can create your own picture of Him in your higher mind, if you can picture the qualities of meekness, humility and love in His face, yours will be a heavenly image. In so creating His picture you will find yourself being drawn right into His heart, and you will live in consciousness of Him and of the spirit life. This in itself will help you to disentangle yourself from the noise and turmoil of the outer world.

NO PRAYER GOES UNANSWERED

There are many methods of healing but there is only one true source from which healing flows. This source is the foundation of life, of love. The Master Jesus' special work is to help humanity reach to the Source of Life. He comes to you whenever you truly call. No prayer ever goes unanswered, because true prayer sets up a vibration in your soul which goes right to the Source of supply. It must be true, sincere prayer, and there must be complete surrender of the soul to God's will.

THE SEEDS OF HEALING
ARE WAITING TO BLOSSOM

Christ the Lord, the Son, is He who draws very near to every human heart which prays in simplicity and humility. Thus the aspirant is quickened at the heart centre, and the seed planted deep in the soil of the soul. In time that soul grows, expands and produces the bloom, the blossom which can only be described as like a rose, the sweetest and most beautiful of flowers. Yes, the rose is the symbol of the Christ life, light and beauty. May the rose bloom in your heart and upon the cross of earthly matter for you.

TENDERNESS

Christ has a heart that knows pain and is deeply burdened; Christ so wisely and so shrewdly human, so wise in His humanity, so deep and broad in compassion; Christ, tender in beauty as a snowdrop, strong, brave and enduring.

4

COME TO ME ... AND I WILL GIVE YOU REST

REST

The Master comes into our midst with His simple message breathed into our hearts now, 'Love one another; and thus fulfill the law of God which is Love'. How surprising it is that when the soul rises above irritations and touches a level of spiritual light and power which is love—that when the soul feels love it is at last at rest. *Come unto me all ye that are weary and heavy-laden, and I will give you rest.*

SEEKING THE CHRIST WITHIN

If your burden is heavy, if you face an ordeal from which you shrink, cease worrying about the future, and strive to visualize the figure who is Love itself. You will instantly be comforted and strengthened. At that moment of contact with supreme Spirit you are touching eternity.

STRONG IN YOUR SELF

You are tired, dear one, and a little unhappy? Will you allow old White Eagle to give you a little advice? There is one source of lasting happiness. This is God. Do not depend upon other people for your happiness. There is a great deal more behind my words, as probably you realize. When you cease to expect and look to others for happiness, you will find you will be overwhelmed with happiness. It will just flow to you from every direction. Centre your attention upon the Great White Spirit and your teacher in spirit. You will receive ample reward.

WHAT YOU ARE EXPERIENCING....

Do not make the mistake of thinking that you are left alone in your difficulties. We are speaking now especially to you who happen to be up against a brick wall, not knowing which way to go or what is going to happen next. You recognize to whom we speak? You are blindfolded, but only for a short period. Contain yourself in confidence and in peace, longing only to be God's servant, praying that you may be still and await His–Her commands. All is known to the agents of the almighty Spirit. No soul is ever left unattended. And yet every soul must pass through its own initiation alone, every soul must pass from one state of life to another alone. It is this very aloneness, this loneliness and mistiness which eventually brings progress to the soul.

... IS INITIATION

You become aware then of a great calm within, and a voice says: 'Lo, I am with you always'. You know this is true. You hear not only our voice speaking; an inner voice is also saying: 'I am the Lord Thy God. Within, my child, *within* is your strength, is the power, is the divine will.' Nothing can happen in your outer physical life that matters more than this, your own initiation into the expansion of the God-consciousness that is yours.

... AND PART OF THE DIVINE PLAN

Human kind unfolds gently and quietly through tribulation and disappointment, through facing and paying its karmic debts courageously. Whatever comes along is a lesson and there is wisdom in the Divine Plan. Nothing happens by chance. The whole of life is governed by divine law, and the law of God is love. God is good and God is love. What shall we say? The art of good living is to accept wisely and with courage, always, what life brings to you: remembering that the chief gift of all is the spirit within yourself.

5

IN THE PRESENCE
OF ANGELS

PROTECTED AND GUIDED

Human kind has always walked the earth with angels. The human race, whether it knows it or not, is still under the guardianship of God's angels. It may strengthen and comfort you to know that not one of you treads the path alone; for from the moment of birth until physical death the soul is guarded by an angel appointed for that task.

RAYS OF LIGHT

As we look into your loving hearts, we see all
the little weaknesses falling away, and only
see that flame, that Divine Light which is
in the heart of your soul. This is what the
angels, the heavenly angels, see. And the
mists are dispelled, the mists of failure are
dispelled. They, your angelic messengers,
come close, close, ever closer to you.

IN COMMUNION

God is your only security. God is omnipotent, and if you would be safe from the enemies of life, place your hand in God's, and trust in divine love. No sickness, no sorrow, no separation, can touch you if you are at one with God in spirit. An angel touches you now. The Master pours down upon you His spirit … His Peace.…

CONCERN FOR THOSE YOU LOVE

When you desire to help others, always make contact with the great Spirit. Then call upon the angels of healing and light. According to how you attune yourself to these great beings, who work in accord with the cosmic laws, they will carry your message to the one you desire to help. Visualize the one you desire to help being held up by the angels of healing, in the Christ Ray.

This unseen force is the mightiest power in the universe—mightier than any human power. It is the Creator. You are as a child, and the teachers of the past have told you human beings that you can do the work of healing, even as the Master Himself healed. Have faith and believe these things, and when things go contrary to *your* wish, remember the Great Spirit holds the plan. Resign yourself, having done all that is in your power, leave the rest to God.

LIGHT SHINES THROUGH ALL

You have the love of the angels within your consciousness, beautifying and healing you, and the light and love of the angels outside your being. They mingle with you, and in the light that you are radiating. All is interwoven into a magnificent blend of life and light.

6

BREATHE IN THE BREATH OF GOD

RELIEF

If you will at this moment relax your mind and body, and quietly and slowly breathe deeply, and as you breathe in, try and imagine that you are breathing in light and life; that you are not only inhaling air; *you are filling every particle of your being with God's Breath.* As you do this, you will naturally be freed from earthly problems because you will forget your body and for a fleeting moment be released. Try it ... for when you thus breathe correctly, you will always find relief from the bondage of cares and limitations.

THE NEW BREATH

We often speak to you of 'breathing in the light'. Now what is the light? The light is harmony. When you try to breathe in the light, you are breathing in harmony and healing; for in the white light are all the colours, made perfect in one.

LIGHT IS LIFE...

There is only one truth, and this is *Light*. It was in the beginning, is now, and ever shall be. Light is your life. When Light is withdrawn, there is no longer any life. The Light within your heart and mind is the only truth; and no matter what takes place on the outer plane, remember, it is illusion, it is passing. The only abiding reality is the Light of God, the Light of your spirit.

...AND LIFE IS LIGHT

All human kind, consciously or unconsciously, is seeking for the Holy Breath. We wonder how many on earth realize its power, which is that of life, of wisdom and of love. May you all search for this Holy Breath. You will find it both in your outer life and in your inner temple. There is much to learn about the art of breathing, which can control your life, your unfoldment and your health on the physical, mental and spiritual planes.

THE TEMPLE OF THE TREES

Let us withdraw to the mountain top …
and within the temple of the pines, with the
canopy of heaven, the stars above, wait to
breathe in the love and blessing of God our
Father, the blessing of God our Mother …
and pray that we may have the will to breathe
out this love and majesty upon all creatures,
upon life. So shall the kingdom of God *become* in us, and the will of God be done in
earth, as it is in heaven.

7

SUNLIGHT
ON YOUR PATH

HEALING IS IN NATURE

Open your souls to the sunlight of God …
a chord which we hope will bring to you
all the harmony of spirit and restoration of
physical strength and health which you need.
You may not realize how much you need the
healing power of God; you may think that
because you are able to carry on your usual
duties, you do not need any healing power at
all. We do assure you that all human beings
need healing, and there are around you the
very healing rays which you need.

WE SHARE OUR JOY WITH YOU

We know how you all feel, we feel your suffering with you, we are sorrowful when you suffer, we feel compassion for you; but oh! how glad we are when we see you respond to God's healing rays! We rejoice when we see that you have touched one of those harmonious chords of life—and you can all touch them.

HARMONY, THE SECRET

The one secret that you must know, and we tell you this many, many times, is harmony in the life. If you want to be well, you must endeavour to live your life in harmony with the divine law of Love. And this means that you do no harm. No suffering must you inflict upon any living creature. Therefore, if you establish this life of harmony and love, your own soul and your own physical body gradually becomes perfect. This is the true secret of all healing. Seek for harmony in your human relationships, love all creatures, love your human companions. Feel in your heart that gentleness of the Master. Love, and your whole body will be recreated, and it will shine in the Light of Heaven.

WHY AM I HERE?

Give all the love, all the light that you have within you. Give it all; broadcast it every moment of your life. In problems at home, problems with your family, problems in your workplace, the answer is to give and give and give that simple light, that pure light of the Son of God which is in your heart. So simple, that pure light of the Son of God which is in your heart! So simple, but so difficult! This is the meaning of all that happens in the material world; and every man, woman and child will have to learn this lesson before they have finished their journey. Every soul will have to learn it because that is why the soul is here on this earth planet.

8

A PATH OF PROGRESS

OPPORTUNITY

We know that daily life can be both sweet and bitter. The outer life brings pleasures which are fleeting, together with periods when great heaviness and darkness seem to fall upon you, and when you seek in vain for comfort and rest. No matter what happenings your karma brings, we would remind you of its import. People resent the teaching of karma. Often they say to us: 'What have I done to deserve this?'; 'Why should this come upon me?' They do not understand that difficulties may be opportunities in disguise. You may not realize that if certain circumstances had *not* come in to your life you would have lacked an opportunity for spiritual growth, a chance of doing certain work; of touching the souls of people brought into contact with you.

SPIRIT IS FREE

The thing is for the spirit to remain unaffected by the challenge—that is the word we will use—the challenge of matter, of the lower life. Strive to respond to beauty and strive to feel love towards life. Let your heart be always in tune with the infinite love.

OUR HOPE FOR YOU

We come with a special message which
we pray will comfort every one of you and
bring spiritual illumination to your souls. By
spiritual illumination we mean health—not
health of body, but health of soul. And health
is holiness. No-one can attain perfect health
without an inner awareness of the Spirit of
the Creator. You must become perfectly balanced between heaven and earth if you are to
be whole and healthy.

BALANCE COMES FROM LOVE

You all need to find balance, and not to be pulled this way and that by your emotions and feelings. On the one hand you must cultivate sympathy, understanding and tolerance, but at the same time you must try to retain a wise and balanced view born of true love.

TOUCH THE HIGHEST WITHIN YOU

Whatever your need—be it physical, spiritual, or material—meditate on the God within, the God which prompts you to live and to act from the very highest motives. You will generate that Light, it will vibrate through your vital body, surrounding you with a great light. It will direct its beams along life's pathway. You will not lack anything you need.

AN EMANATION FROM WITHIN

To heal sick bodies is good, but to heal the soul is better. When your heart is full of love and compassion, you are sending out from your own centre the light which God has implanted in you as a tiny seed. As you aspire to the Great White Spirit, God, so this light and power grows in you. Every thought of God, every small effort that you make to think rightly, to reach up to the higher level of truth, goodness, purity and love, is helping to heal the world. This manifestation of sunlight through you, the quiet infiltration of this holy light into human hearts and lives, will indeed heal the *whole* world.

9

COURAGE! KEEP STEADILY ON

YOUR DESTINY IS GLORIOUS

Our message to you is, 'Let the Light shine!'
Be not weary in well-doing. Pray for courage and keep steadily on, serving according
to your capacity on the physical, mental and
spiritual planes, all three according to where
you are placed. You have nothing to fear, but
everything to look forward to, to live for, to
strive for. O my brethren, a glorious life is
the destiny of all God's children!

UNBOUNDED FREEDOM

Sometimes, in the physical life, many trials are set before you. Sometimes you feel worry, or your heart seems to be breaking. This of course is the result of physical life and the training every soul has to go through. But you will find with each triumph over the difficulties, the problems, the hurts and disappointments in your life, even if it appears insignificant, that you will make a big step forward on your path towards freedom. You cannot know yet what that freedom means to a soul.

THE ROAD TO JOY

We can only assure you that what seems to you a tragedy will eventually reveal itself as a wonderful opportunity—an opportunity for you to learn, and to develop spiritual powers which will eventually remove you from all the anguish, the frustration, the hurts and disappointments of physical life. A soul can only learn these lessons and get this training through living on the earth plane in a physical body. You can't be born into heaven and have everything honey and cream and strawberries. That's no good to you at all! You have to learn to accept what is given to you to bring forth the God in you, so that you deal with life in a godly way. And, remember, the angels are ever ready to come to your aid.

A PERFECT EXAMPLE

We hold before you the life of the Master Jesus … such a simple, pure, holy life. But it was a remarkable demonstration of how life ought to be lived in the physical body: a life of sacrifice and service, a life of love, but a life in which he had also to be stern and strong. Don't think that love means you've always got to be easy-going and soft. There are times when you have to grip a situation with courage and determination, and with trust and faith in the Great Spirit.

REALIZE YOUR INNER STRENGTH

The purpose of your incarnation is to become stronger and stronger in spiritual light and power, so that you may bring through into daily life the radiance of your spiritual life. We know your difficulties; we know how the physical body holds you fast in its grip, and through it you suffer fears and pains, disorder of mind and spirit. In the words of the Master Jesus, we say, *Rise up; take up your bed*—which is the material life; *rise up and walk.* Walk the spiritual path, the path of light. When you get this inner contact with the true source of your being, hold fast. Strive, and triumph over the darkness of physical matter!

TRUST

God's plan is perfect. Why then do you allow
yourself to become so anxious and worried?
Nothing happens by chance; all is ordered by
divine law. When one 'sins' or breaks spiritual
law, the result of this foolishness is always
put to good use by divine law. Thus God is
always repairing, always healing the nations,
always healing souls, and though it may seem
to you certain things happen by chance, in
fact everything works together according to
the divine will. Always remember this, and
having done your best with the material at
hand, surrender the rest to the divine love
and perfect law.

THE OPENING BUD

All your experiences are intended to bring to you a deeper understanding. Your sufferings, your love, your pains, all unfold the Rose of Christ within your heart.

THE LOVE WITHIN WILL TRIUMPH

Whatever the circumstances of life, however drab and weary life may appear, if the heart within the child of God is aware of the spirit and purpose of life and aware of its love for all beings, then it knows joy. It knows a contentment of which nothing can rob the soul.

10

NEVER LOSE HOPE!

A MESSAGE WHEN LIFE SEEMS HARD

To those who are sick, we come to help you help yourselves. Every soul must attune itself to the infinite power, Love. Love is the worker of miracles. Divine love will meet every need that you have. The material world and the physical body may seem to you a very hard condition, and you become accustomed to thinking in terms of pain and inconvenience and ills of the flesh; they seem so obstinate and will not be removed. Of course they will not, if you think about them; but as soon as you dwell in spirit, in the vibrations of the Father—Mother and the Christ you will feel the inflow of a magic power of healing. Do not be in too much of a hurry. Be patient. Never lose hope, never lose faith.

OVERCOMING LIMITATION....

Many of you are frustrated in your daily life because things will not go the way you want them to, and you become disillusioned with our teaching about God's love. But we would assure you that as you daily strive to overcome all doubts—about the love and the wisdom of God—you will be getting nearer and nearer to that expansion of your own consciousness. You will feel and be blessed with heavenly joy, comfort and assurance that in God's world *all is well*.

...IS HEALING FOR THE SOUL

We ask you to banish all thought of disability. Do not dwell upon disease: you are with God, you are part of God. You, the spirit, must raise your consciousness above the body. Banish the arguments of the reasoning, earthly mind, for it has the power to subject you to the darkness of materialism; but the Christ, the seed within your heart, has the power to raise you up out of the limitations of physical matter. The healing of the soul is far more important than that of the body. In the calmness of your spirit, try and retain the peace of heaven. Surrender yourself to the infinite love, wisdom and power of the

Divine Master, the Great Healer, and then you cannot fail to breathe in the breath of God and go forth to live in harmony with God's law—Love.

A HIGHER PHYSICIAN

Sometimes when you see your dear ones suffering pain or serious sickness, you are heartbroken and torn with their suffering; but do you not think your Father–Mother knows what that dear one is going through and what the soul needs? Is not God the greatest physician known to human kind? God gently administers the healing power to that soul. You are God's children, and the Son, the Lord Christ, gathers you into the great family.

WALK YOUR OWN PATH
IN LOVING SIMPLICITY

There is nothing to fear, beloved. Nothing to
fear except fear. White Eagle will give you a
word of caution, however, if you will receive
it. Never try to carry burdens which are not
yours. That will sound strange for us to tell
you. But it is better to help your brother or
your sister to put the burdens on his or her
own back. Encourage, sympathize; but you
cannot carry anyone else's burden, because
cosmic law says each soul must bear its own.
Work for God in harmony with God's laws.
Let God strengthen you in all you do. Never
let the material burdens of others crush you.

If you do, you will be incapacitated for the service of the Master. It is a very subtle point, my dear ones, to learn how to walk the middle way, to give sympathy and true help but not to be pulled over into the chaos of the lower realms.

11

SERENITY

WITH A TRANQUIL MIND AND HEART

We would emphasize the great need there is for all souls who aspire to the Great Spirit above to learn the secret and the power of a tranquil and serene mind. Serenity is one of the most important conditions to which men and women, placed in the vortex of human life, can attain. We advise you who are loved of the Father and of the Mother to pray daily in the turmoil of your earthly life for calmness of mind and heart. When you have found a degree of calmness, you will not find it difficult to feel love. May this be your daily prayer: 'O God, may Thy Glory and Light give me a calm mind; and may Thy spirit give unto me love!'.

RELAXATION

Do not neglect times of relaxation. When you relax, you are giving yourselves, your bodies, the time needed to be recharged, replenished. We know that the demands of life at the present time are very strong—we are going to say also very tempting—but do remember to relax whenever you can. By 'relax' we mean just going to God, tuning yourself into God-consciousness, and going easy. Slacken off the tension in the physical body. Go into your place of knowledge, your awareness that all is well.

EVERY CHILD OF GOD IS
ALSO AN AGENT OF GOD

The light of your lamp shines forth more brightly when you are serene, when you have learnt to control the passions of fear, anger and hatred. You must learn to reach these spheres of serenity continually, for there lies the power of good. It is through the children of earth that God works miracles.

THE STILL SMALL VOICE OF CALM

'To seek the place of serenity and peace': this is the desire of every soul. And the turbulence of the earth is to teach you the way to find serenity. This is difficult for those on earth to understand, but the soul must pass through the fires of passion until they are burnt out. The soul must pass over turbulent seas of human emotion until the emotions learn to be still at the call of the Master, Christ.

12

DEATH: RELEASE
INTO THE LIGHT

A MAGICAL THOUGHT TO HOLD

The one thing which will help you in crossing the bridge between this earth plane and the next world is positive thought of God, of light. Whenever the time comes for you yourself to arise out of mortal life, hold in your mind, throughout this experience, this one supreme thought: 'God, my Father, my Mother, my beloved! I am in Thee, Thou art in me, and I cannot die, I go forth into the freer and grander life'.

DEATH IS AN OPENING

When people leave the physical body at death—after their spirit, pure spirit, has withdrawn from the entanglements of the physical body—they are in that world of loveliness which we have endeavoured to help you feel for a flash. They are in that world of wonderful movement and music and harmony and perfection. They feel so light and so happy. Their movements are so free and they hear the heavenly music. Think, when you lose a loved one by death, that this is what they go to: they are cleansed and purified of all the pain and suffering and anguish of the earthly life. They are free! You know, the angel comes to draw the bolts of the prison house and the spirit goes forth—so free to the joy and happiness which it has earned through its life on the physical plane!

IMAGINE THE HEAVENLY GARDEN

Is it not beautiful and comforting to know that a heavenly garden for rest and refreshment and communion with your loved ones awaits you after the long 'day' on earth? Try to use your imagination. Don't allow yourselves to be so tightly held down to earth. Imagine what it could be like to enter that heavenly garden and meet again friends whom you thought you had lost. It's a lovely thought, isn't it?—but, we assure you, it is a more lovely thing to experience.

A WAY OF LIFE

This is truth; it is so simple: just *live and love and have faith; believe, aspire and do good.* It is as simple as that. Then all is beauty. There is no death. In that cup, in that sacrament, you are united for ever with loved ones. No-one is ever lost. Your dear one is with you now in form, as close as ever. It is now the finest and the most beautiful part of them that is close to you, for the dross has been melted away and there only remains the pure gold of the Christ Spirit which is within us all.

LOVE WELCOMES YOU

You can never be separated from those you love, so long as you love them, and you love God; *you are all one….*

ALL IS ONE

Death and birth are both in God, and both are beautiful, with nothing to dread in either experience, but everything to welcome.

THE LORD IS MY SHEPHERD

May the Great Lord above bless you and sustain you for all your days on earth, and gently shepherd you into the soul world of golden light.

BEFORE SLEEP:
A HEALING MEDITATION

Now close your eyes, close your senses to all
earthly things; come with us in spirit and
see that we have brought you into a Temple
of Healing, indescribable in earth language.
All we can tell you is that it is radiating all
the colours of the spectrum, gentle, sweet
colours. Shall we liken it to a pearl?

We are in the temple of the pearl ray; its
tall columns rise right up into the heaven....
But it isn't so much the perfection of the ar-

chitecture that impresses us, as the perfect harmony and beauty that we feel....

Imagine this perfect healing temple, and you will see it; you will feel the glory of this life here in spirit. It is for you, it is part of you, my child.... How can you be anxious and worried about earthly things, when you have seen and know that true life, which is working all things together to produce good in human kind?

Try to live in this consciousness always, always. Withdraw from the noise and the babble of the outer world. Go into this temple, kneel in simple prayer before the communion table and receive from your Lord and Master the sacrament ... the bread and the wine.

*

Rise with renewed strength and go forward, in company with your loved ones in spirit. Even if your work is of a very material nature, in a very worldly world, even in this you are helped and guided. Never forget that each one of you is watched over. Your soul-need is known. So open your heart in simple trust, and all the crooked places will be made straight.

With all our love we leave you. Have courage, have faith, never doubt the love and wisdom of your Creator.